A Guide for Using

Too Much Noise

in the Classroom

Based on the novel written by Ann McGovern

This guide written by Sandy Pellow

WESTERN EDUCATIONAL ACTIVITIES LTD.
12006 - 111 Ave. Edmonton, Alberta T5G 0E6
Ph: (780) 413-7055   Fax: (780) 413-7055
GST # R105636187

Teacher Created Materials, Inc.
6421 Industry Way
Westminster, CA 92683
www.teachercreated.com

©1996 Teacher Created Materials, Inc.
Reprinted, 1999

Made in U.S.A.

ISBN1-55734-568-6

Edited by
Mary Kaye Taggart

Illustrated by
Howard Chaney

Cover Art by
Wendy Chang

Table of Contents

Introduction and Sample Lessons

A good book can touch the lives of children like a good friend. The pictures, words, and characters can inspire young minds as they turn to literary treasures for companionship, recreation, comfort, and guidance. Great care has been taken in selecting the books and unit activities that comprise the primary series of *Literature Units*. Teachers who use this literature unit to supplement their own valuable ideas can plan the activities, using one of the following methods.

Sample Lesson Plan

The sample lessons below provide the teacher with a specific set of lesson plan suggestions. Each of the lessons can take from one to several days to complete and can include all or some of the suggested activities. Refer to the "Suggestions for Using the Unit Activities" on pages 6–11 for information relating to the unit activities.

Unit Planner

For the teacher who wishes to tailor the suggestions on pages 6–11 in a format other than that prescribed in the Sample Lesson Plan, a blank unit planner is provided on page four. On a specific day you may choose the activities you wish to include by writing the activity number or a brief notation about the activity. Space has been provided for reminders, comments, and other pertinent information relating to each day's activities. Reproduce copies of the Unit Planner as needed.

Sample Lesson Plan

Lesson 1

- Read *Crash! Bang! Boom!* by Peter Spier to the class.
- Display "Sounds on My Street" poem on chart paper. (page 18)
- Complete group activity 4 on page 6.
- Sing "Old MacDonald Had a Farm."
- Play vocabulary word game. (pages 26 and 27)
- Make leaf fans. (page 28)
- Begin practice for Readers' Theater. (pages 36-46)
- Practice vocabulary words for pocket chart. (page 7, activity 11)

Lesson 2

- Read *Sounds* by J. Douglas Lee to the class.
- Lead a discussion on sounds and noises.
- Read *Too Much Noise* to the class.
- Learn and recite the sounds poem. (page 19)
- Complete the small group activity. (page 8, activity 1)
- Complete the large group listening activity. (page 8, activity 2)
- Lead discussion on problem solving.
- Read *But No Elephants* by Jerry Smath to the class.

- Make masks and work on the Readers' Theater play. (pages 36–46)
- Read "About the Author." (page 5)

Lesson 3

- Fill in Peter's thought cloud. (page 29)
- Complete the pocket chart activities. (pages 12–14)
- Fill in the story frame. (page 30)
- Recall the story sequence. (page 31)
- Prepare stick puppets and theater. (pages 20–23)
- Practice the Readers' Theater play.

Lesson 4

- Do the sentence strips activities. (pages 16 and 17)
- Complete quotation marks pocket chart lesson. (pages 32 and 33)
- Make an animal flip book. (page 24)
- Practice following directions. (page 25)
- Continue practicing Readers' Theater play.

Lesson 5

- Make sugar cookies. (page 11)
- Complete word problems. (page 34)
- Investigate sounds. (page 35)
- Make leaf prints. (page 10, activity 8)
- Complete the culminating activity. (page 11)

Unit Planner

Date	Unit Activities	Date	Unit Activities
Notes/Comments:		Notes/Comments:	
Date	Unit Activities	Date	Unit Activities
Notes/Comments:		Notes/Comments:	
Date	Unit Activities	Date	Unit Activities
Notes/Comments:		Notes/Comments:	

Getting to Know the Book and Author

About the Book

(Too Much Noise is published in the U.S.A. by Houghton Mifflin Company. It is also available in Canada from Thomas Allen and Son, in U.K. from Cassell, and in Australia from Jackaranda Wiley.)

Peter is an old man who lives in an old, old house. His bed creaks, his floor squeaks, his teakettle whistles, and the leaves fall on the roof. All these things are too noisy for Peter, so he decides to visit the village wise man for advice on how to get rid of the noises.

The wise man gives him some very unusual advice. First, he tells him to get a cow, then a donkey, a sheep, and many other animals in succession. Each animal makes a lot more noise than the previous ones. Eventually, his house becomes so noisy and crowded with all the animals that Peter thinks he will go crazy, so he goes back to the wise man.

The wise man's solution is to remove the animals one by one until all the noises or sounds that remain are the creak of the bed, the squeak of the floor, the whistle of the teakettle, and the sound of the leaves falling on the roof. Even though these are the same sounds that Peter thought were so noisy at first, he now thinks these are very quiet sounds.

About the Author

Ann McGovern, author of more than 50 books for children, has great enthusiasm for life. This enthusiasm is evident in all her books, which open new worlds to young readers. McGovern began writing as a young girl. She had a childhood stutter which kept her from expressing herself orally, so she turned to expressing her feelings and thoughts by writing. She spent her childhood years in New York City's public library or in Central Park, writing poems and stories.

Her vast personal experiences carry over as topics in her books. She is a world traveler, a photographer, a scuba diver, and a lifelong pursuer of knowledge. Topics in her books range from riding elephants to photographing tigers in India. One of her great loves is scuba diving, which has inspired quite a few stories about underwater adventures. She also enjoys writing biographies about people who are good role models for children.

In addition to biographies, nature books, and histories, McGovern writes picture books, adapts folktales, writes novels, and composes poetry. As for her poetry, she always strives to write verse that is meaningful to children. In recent years many of her ideas for books have come from her grandchildren.

Too Much Noise, one of her earliest endeavors, was published in 1967.

Suggestions for Using the Unit Activities

Use some or all of the following activities to help children understand and appreciate the story, as well as to introduce, reinforce, and extend skills across the curriculum. The suggested activities have been divided into three sections to assist the teacher in planning the literature unit.

The sections are as follows:

- **Before the Book** includes suggestions for preparing the classroom environment and the students for the literature to be read.
- **Into the Book** has activities that focus on the book's content, characters, theme, etc.
- **After the Book** extends the reader's enjoyment of the book.

Before the Book

1. Complete the following projects before you begin the unit:

   - Record sounds of everyday things for the listening game described on page 8.
   - Make cookie dough, using the recipe on page 11. Store the dough in the refrigerator.
   - Get a whistling teakettle and some tea bags.
   - Copy the poems (pages 18 and 19) onto tagboard or chart paper.
   - Prepare vocabulary cards, story questions, and sentence strips for the pocket chart activities. (Directions and patterns are provided on pages 12–17.)

2. Read Peter Spier's *Crash! Bang! Boom!* (Doubleday, 1972) to the class. This story introduces children to a vast vocabulary of sound words. Discuss the words that they like in the book. Show students how many of the words have distinctive sounds when they say them aloud.

3. Read the poem on page 18 to the class. Have children share the words they like in the poem. Discuss sounds they hear in their neighborhood or homes.

4. Discuss sounds and noises. Divide the class into four groups. Send each group to a corner of the room. On chart paper, have each group write a list of these sounds: group 1—nice (or pleasant) sounds, group 2—bad (or irritating) sounds, group 3—loud sounds, group 4—soft sounds. After the groups are done, ask each group to select a spokesperson to read the list of sounds. Keep the four charts on display in the room during the week.

5. Read *Sounds* by J. Douglas Lee to the class. Talk about sounds that are heard in each room of the house. Then discuss sounds that are heard in the classroom (voices, pencils being sharpened, bells, etc.).

6. Sing "Old MacDonald Had a Farm." Have children add as many farm animals as possible. The masks on pages 41–46 can be used during the singing. Vary this activity by changing the theme of the song from a farm to a zoo or a jungle. Ask children to name other animals that would fit these categories.

Suggestions for Using the Unit Activities *(cont.)*

Before the Book *(cont.)*

7. Introduce the vocabulary game on pages 26 and 27. This game can be played individually or with partners. First read all the animal names and the sounds they make. Instruct the children to cut apart the vocabulary sheet into individual animal and sound cards. Put all the animal cards in one pile and all the sound cards in another. If students work in pairs, have one child read the animal card name and ask the other child to choose the sound it makes. After all the animals and sounds are matched, students can trade places. The cards can be kept in resealable plastic storage bags and played throughout the week. Other games are suggested on page 27.

8. Have students make leaf fans. Leaf patterns are provided on page 28. Provide three or more leaves for each child. (Use fall colors.) Have students print a different vocabulary or spelling word on each leaf. They then cut out the leaves. A leaf fan is formed by attaching the leaves at the stems with a brass fastener and spreading them out to form a fan. Students can keep the leaf fans at their desks for vocabulary practice activities during the week.

9. Prepare materials ahead of time for the Readers' Theater presentation (pages 36–46). Reproduce the script pages and prepare a script booklet, as shown on page 37. At an appropriate time, choose twelve children for the speaking parts. Assign other students to help with the play. (See suggestions on page 36). Plan time in your unit schedule to practice the play, make masks and props, and present the Readers' Theater.

10. Prepare a bulletin board. Use the suggestion on page 47 or create your own. You may wish to involve students in the preparation.

11. Discuss the following words in context before reading the story. Make several copies of the leaf pattern on page 14. Write the words below on the leaves. Display the leaves on a pocket chart. (See page 12 for directions on making a pocket chart.)

angry	crazy	leaves
creak	quiet	house
squeak	dream	wind
whistle	floor	through
village	roof	
noisy	blew	

Suggestions for Using the Unit Activities *(cont.)*

Into the Book

1. Read the poem on page 19 to the class. Provide students with a copy of the poem, place the copy on an overhead projector, or write it on chart paper. Reread the poem and ask the children to make a list of other words that could replace those in the poem. As an extension, have the children work in small groups to create a fourth stanza for the poem. Another activity is suggested at the bottom of page 19. Ask groups to share their ideas with the rest of the class.

2. Have students complete the following listening activity. Divide the class into two teams. Play recorded sounds of everyday things (one at a time). Assign a spokesperson to announce the answers for each team. If a team's answer is correct, the team gets a point. If an answer is incorrect, the opposing team gets a chance to guess the same sound. The team with the most points wins.

   These are the sounds that need to be recorded ahead of time.

running faucet water	zipper	lawn mower
sprinkler	tearing paper	opening a soda can
shower	ticking clock	sound of a blender
creaking door	banging 2 lids together	whistling teakettle
clapping hands	typewriter clicking	electric pencil sharpener
snapping fingers	door slamming	toilet flushing
blowing whistle	car engine starting	knocking at a door
bouncing ball		

3. Read Jerry Smath's *But No Elephants* to the class. This story is about problem solving. Lead a class discussion on ways to solve problems. Problems that arise on the playground, in the classroom, or at home might be topics of discussion.

4. Read the biography of Ann McGovern (page 5) to the class. Collect as many Ann McGovern books as possible to show the children the great variety of topics she has written about.

5. Write the following questions on the board. Ask students to think about them as you read *Too Much Noise* to the class.
   - Who are the main characters?
   - Which parts of the story are repeated?
   - Why does the wise man give Peter the advice he does?
   - What made the wise man wise?

6. Develop critical thinking skills with the story questions on page 15. The questions are based on Bloom's Taxonomy and are provided in each of Bloom's Levels of Learning. Reproduce several copies of the teakettle on page 14. Use the teakettle patterns for the story question activities described on page 13.

7. After reading *Too Much Noise*, distribute page 29 to the class. Ask the children to draw or write in the cloud above Peter's head as many of the things that were bothering Peter as they can remember. Have students share their responses with the class.

Suggestions for Using the Unit Activities *(cont.)*

Into the Book *(cont.)*

8. Have students complete the story frame on page 30. Guide them as they fill in the frame. This activity will help them see the sequence of the whole story by retelling the main events. This can be done as a whole class or in small groups.

9. Distribute copies of the story sequence activity on page 31. Ask children to fill in the clouds by writing the main events of the story in order. If students find this too difficult to complete independently, model the activity first. Discuss the main events of the story, writing them in order, starting with number one and going clockwise around the circle. This will require much teacher direction for very young students.

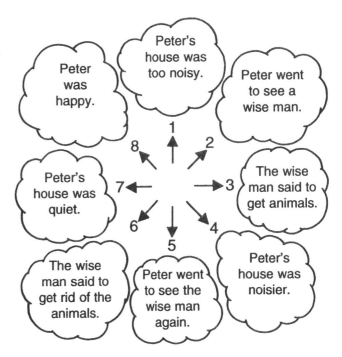

10. Prepare stick puppet theaters, following the suggestions and directions on page 20. Allow the students to construct puppets by coloring, cutting, and gluing puppets on tongue depressors. Use the suggestions for stick puppets on page 21.

After the Book

1. Refer to the sentences on pages 16 and 17 to prepare story summary sentence strips. Cut out the sentence strips. Laminate a set of sentences for use with a pocket chart. Work with students on some or all of the following activities.

   • On the pocket chart, place the sentences in the order in which the events happened in the story.

   • Use the sentences to retell the story.

   • Divide the class into small groups and distribute a few sentence strips to each group. Ask the groups to act out the part of the story represented by the sentence.

   In addition to these activities, you may wish to reproduce the pages and have students read the sentences aloud to partners or take them home to read to parents, siblings, etc.

2. Introduce or review the use of quotation marks to indicate dialogue. Refer to the use of quotation marks used in *Too Much Noise*. Model examples for the class and provide student practice. Prepare a pocket chart activity, using the sentence words and quotation marks on pages 32 and 33. Reproduce the pages on index paper and then cut out the strips. Or, the words and quotation marks can be transferred onto tagboard strips. Using the pocket chart, ask children to place the quotation marks in the appropriate places in the sentences.

Suggestions for Using the Unit Activities *(cont.)*

After the Book *(cont.)*

3. Have children create animal flip books. Follow the directions on page 24. Children draw the head, body, and tail of any animal in the appropriate section of the page. Under each section they write WHO it is, WHAT it is doing, and WHERE or WHEN the action occurs. Create the sections by cutting vertically on the dotted lines. Staple all pages together at the top to form either an individual book or a class flip book.

4. Prepare masks (pages 41-46) to use for the Readers' Theater. These masks can also be used for extension activities you may wish to include in the unit. Allow children who do not have parts in the theater production to cut out and color the masks for the play.

5. Have children practice following directions. Distribute page 25 and ask students to complete Peter's house by following the directions at the bottom of the page. Depending on the reading level of the class, this activity can be assigned as independent practice or as a teacher directed page.

6. Distribute page 34. Model a few problems for the students before assigning this page as an independent or partner activity. Answers are provided at the bottom of page 34.

7. Use the activities on page 35 to investigate sound.

   All Steamed Up!: A whistling teakettle and an electric burner are needed for the lesson on steam. This lesson consists of class discussions on the three forms of water (solid, liquid, and gas). Showing the three forms of water to the students makes this idea more tangible. Demonstrate how boiling the water in the teakettle makes steam. Also have some ice cubes available to show the solid form of water.

   Investigating Sounds: Several activities are listed which will help the students sharpen their listening skills.

8. Make leaf prints. These can be done on paper or fabric and then mounted and displayed in the classroom. Collect leaves of different sizes and shapes. Paint one side of the leaf (craft paint works well) and press it down on paper or a piece of material. Lift it off carefully by the stem, and the shape of the leaf will make a nice design. Choose a new leaf and paint it with a different color. Repeat this several times, sometimes overlapping, and an attractive pattern develops. After the paint dries, mount the designs on a darker background paper for display.

Suggestions for Using the Unit Activities *(cont.)*

After the Book *(cont.)*

9. Pull the unit together with a culminating activity that features the Readers' Theater and its related activities.

   Present the Readers' Theater. Suggestions for preparing and presenting the Readers' Theater are provided on page 36. Use the Readers' Theater Script (pages 38–40) to involve the students in a dramatic interpretation of the story. The masks on pages 41–46 can be used during the presentation.

   Prepare for and practice the script often before the end of the unit. You may wish to reproduce the invitation on page 36 and invite other classes and parents to see the play. Display any other related projects the children did during the unit. Prepare cookies (see recipe below) and tea ahead of time. Serve as refreshments after the play.

Sugar Cookie Recipe

This can be done in class with help from the children, or the teacher or parent volunteers many want to make dough at home. Use leaf or animal cookie cutters to go with the story.

Ingredients:

- 1 ¼ cups (310 mL) sugar
- 2 eggs
- 1 tablespoon (15 mL) vanilla
- ¾ teaspoon (3.8 mL) baking powder
- ½ teaspoon (2.5 mL) salt

- 1 cup (250 mL) shortening
- ¼ cup (60 mL) light corn syrup
- 3 cups (750 mL) all-purpose flour
- ½ teaspoon (2.5 mL) baking soda

Directions:

Heat oven to 375° Fahrenheit (190° Celsius).

Combine sugar and shortening in a large bowl. Using an electric mixer, beat them together at medium speed until well blended. Add the eggs, syrup, and vanilla. Beat well. Combine the flour, baking powder, baking soda, and salt. Add the dry mixture gradually to the creamed mixture at low speed. Mix until well blended. If the dough is sticky/soft, refrigerate it for one hour. Spread some flour on a flat surface. Roll the dough to 1/4-inch (.6 cm) thickness. Cut shapes out with floured cookie cutters. Transfer them to an ungreased baking sheet.

Bake the cookies for five to nine minutes. Do not overbake. Cool them for two minutes on a baking sheet. Remove the baking sheet to a counter to completely cool and then frost if desired.

This recipe makes about three to four dozen cookies, depending on their size.

Pocket Chart Activities

A pocket chart can be used to hold the vocabulary cards (page 7, activity 11), the story questions (page 15), and the sentence strips (pages 16 and 17).

How to Make a Pocket Chart

If a commercial pocket chart is unavailable, you can make a pocket chart if you have access to a laminator. Begin by laminating a 24" x 36" (60 cm x 90 cm) piece of colored tagboard. Run about 20" (50 cm) of additional plastic. To make nine pockets, cut the clear plastic into nine equal strips. Space the strips equally down the 36" (90 cm) length of the tagboard. Attach each strip with cellophane tape along the bottom and sides. This will hold sentence strips, word cards, etc., and can be displayed in a learning center or mounted on a chalk tray for use by a group. When your pocket chart is ready, use it to display the sentence strips, vocabulary words, and question cards. A sample chart is provided below.

How to Use the Pocket Chart

1. Make vocabulary cards by reproducing the leaf pattern on page 14. Write vocabulary words on the leaves (see the vocabulary list on page 7). Use these vocabulary words to familiarize the children with difficult words and their meanings by giving them context clues. The leaf pattern can also be enlarged and used to make student awards titled "Radical Reader" or "Wonderful Worker."

house   wind   roof   leaves   floor

sentence strip

How many animals are in this story?

sentence strip

Why did Peter visit a wise man?

sentence strip

If a tea kettle was whistling, where was it sitting?

sentence strip

How do you think the wise man became so wise?

Pocket Chart Activities *(cont.)*

How to Use the Pocket Chart

2. Reproduce several copies of the teakettle pattern (page 14) on six different colors of construction paper. Use one color of paper to represent each of Bloom's Levels of Learning.

For example:

    I. Knowledge (green)

    II. Comprehension (orange)

    III. Application (yellow)

    IV. Analysis (red)

    V. Synthesis (purple)

    VI. Evaluation (blue)

Write a question from page 15 on the appropriate color-coded teakettle. Write the level of the question on the lid. Laminate the teakettle for durability.

After reading *Too Much Noise*, provide opportunities for the children to develop and practice higher level critical thinking skills by using the questions on the color-coded teakettles with some or all of the following activities:

- Use a specified color-coded set of teakettles to question students at a particular level of learning.

- Have a child choose a card, read it aloud, or give it to the teacher to read aloud. The child can answer the question or call on a volunteer to answer it.

- Pair children. The teacher reads a question. Children take turns responding to the question.

- Play a game. Divide the class into teams. Ask for a response to a question from one of the question cards. Teams score a point for each appropriate response.

3. Use sentence strips to practice oral reading and sequencing of the story events. Reproduce pages 16 and 17. If possible, laminate them for durability. Cut out the sentence strips or prepare

> Peter's house was quiet now, even though the bed creaked, the floor squeaked, the leaves swished, and the teakettle hissed.

4. Use pages 32 and 33 to conduct a lesson on the use of quotation marks. Words from the sentences should be transferred onto tagboard strips for use in the pocket chart. Students then place the quotation marks in the appropriate places in the sentences.

Pocket Chart Patterns

See pages 12 and 13 for directions.

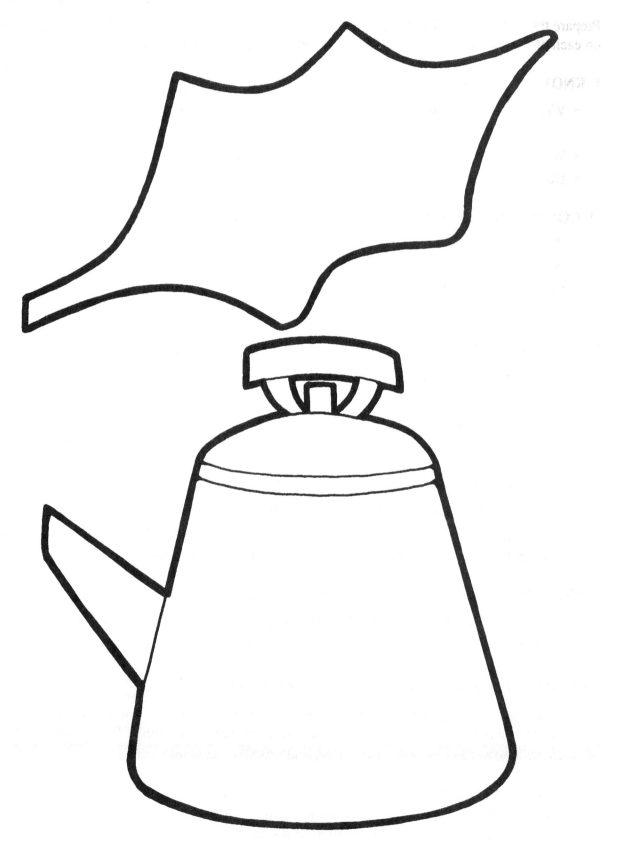

Story Questions

The following questions are based on Bloom's Levels of Learning

Prepare the teakettles as directed on page 13. Write a different question from the Levels of Learning on each of the teakettles. Use the teakettles with the suggested activities.

I. KNOWLEDGE (ability to recall learned information)

- What was the problem with Peter's house?
- Who did Peter visit in the village about his noisy house?
- What made the noise "swish, swish"?
- How many animals are in this story?

II. COMPREHENSION (basic understanding of information)

- Why did Peter's bed creak and his floor squeak?
- Why did Peter visit a wise man?
- Do you think the wise man gave Peter good advice?
- Which of the animals do you think would be the noisiest? the quietest?

III. APPLICATION (ability to do something new with information)

- Did Peter understand why the wise man wanted him to put animals in his house?
- If the teakettle was whistling, where was it sitting?
- What do you think Peter was going to make with the water in the teakettle?
- Why do you think it is hard to do your homework in a very noisy room?

IV. ANALYSIS (ability to examine the parts of a whole)

- How do you think the wise man became so wise?
- Why do you think the "swish" of leaves and the "hiss" of the teakettle bothered Peter so much?
- What bothers you more—high, squeaky sounds or loud, low sounds?

V. SYNTHESIS (ability to bring together information to make something new)

- Besides animals, what else could the wise man have used to teach Peter a lesson?
- Why are some people afraid of thunder and lightning?

VI. EVALUATION (ability to form and defend an opinion)

- Do you think Peter would ever go back to the wise man for advice? Why or why not?
- Do you think the noises in Peter's house will ever bother him again? Why or why not?
- Would you recommend this story to a friend? Why or why not?

Story Summary Sentence Strips

See page 9 (activity 1) for directions.

Peter lived in an old, old house.

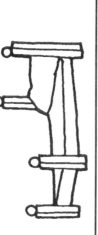

The bed creaked and the floor squeaked.

The leaves went "swish." The teakettle went "hiss."

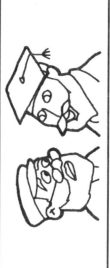

Peter went to see the wise man of the village about his noisy house.

The wise man told Peter to get many animals and take them into his house.

Story Summary Sentence Strips *(cont.)*

See page 9 (activity 1) for directions.

Peter got a cow, and then a donkey, a sheep, a hen, a dog, and a cat.

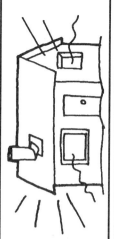

All these animals made Peter's house noisier than ever.

Peter went back to the wise man to complain about all the noise.

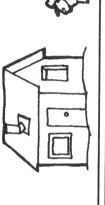

The wise man told Peter to remove the animals from his house one at a time.

Peter's house was quiet now, even though the bed creaked, the floor squeaked, the leaves swished, and the teakettle hissed.

Poetry Fun

Sounds on My Street

Up and down the street I go—What is that I hear?
Sounds and noises everywhere—floating in my ear.

Dogs barking, cats howling, children screaming as they play.
Car horns honking, sirens wailing, sprinklers spraying all the day.

Mamas singing, papas talking, music blaring through the walls.
Chainsaws buzzing, branches falling, big boys bouncing basketballs.

Girls skating, boys jumping, seesaws going up and down.
Babies crying, strollers squeaking, traffic going into town.

Walking, walking—I am walking—greeting friends that I meet.
Sounds and noises as I'm walking—up and down my street.

Poetry Fun *(cont.)*

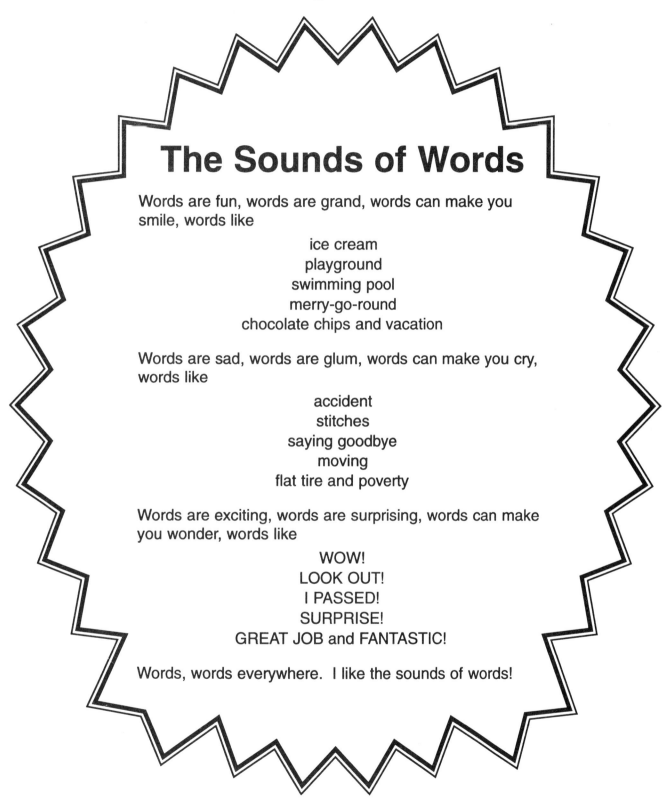

The Sounds of Words

Words are fun, words are grand, words can make you smile, words like

ice cream
playground
swimming pool
merry-go-round
chocolate chips and vacation

Words are sad, words are glum, words can make you cry, words like

accident
stitches
saying goodbye
moving
flat tire and poverty

Words are exciting, words are surprising, words can make you wonder, words like

WOW!
LOOK OUT!
I PASSED!
SURPRISE!
GREAT JOB and FANTASTIC!

Words, words everywhere. I like the sounds of words!

Note to the Teacher: After reading the above poem about words, have students get together in four groups and make their own lists of words. Each group should make a different list (examples: happy words, sad words, exciting words, silly words). After an allotted time, ask each group to share its list with the rest of the class. Post the lists in the room so that all can enjoy.

Stick Puppet Theater

Make a class set of puppet theaters (one for each child) or make one theater for every two to four children. Stick puppet patterns and directions for making stick puppets are provided on pages 21–23.

Materials:

- 22" x 28" (56 cm x 71 cm) pieces of colored poster board (enough for each student or group of students)

- markers, crayons, or paint

- scissors or craft knife

Directions: Fold the poster board 8" (20 cm) in from each of the shorter sides. (See the picture below.) Cut a "window" in the front panel, large enough to accommodate two or three stick puppets. Let the children personalize and decorate their own theaters. Laminate the stick puppet theaters to make them more durable. You may wish to send the theaters home at the end of the year or save them to use year after year.

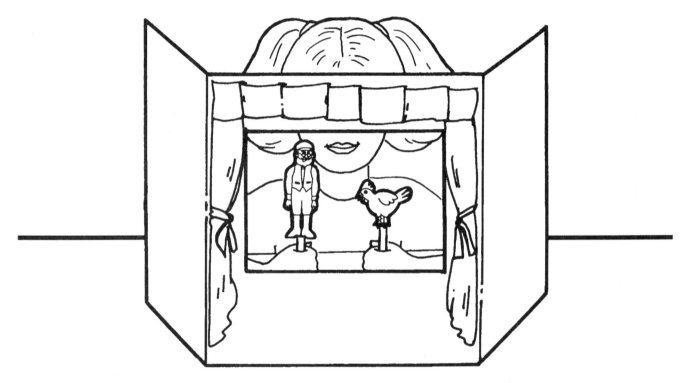

Consider the following suggestions for using the puppets and puppet theaters:

- Prepare the stick puppets, using the directions on this page. Use the puppets and the puppet theaters with the Readers' Theater script on pages 38–40. (Let small groups of children take turns reading the parts and using the stick puppets.)

- Let the children experiment with the puppets by telling the story in their own words or reading from the book.

- As you make statements about the characters in the book, have children hold up the correct stick puppets. Read a statement from the story and have students hold up the stick puppet that represents who or what might have said it.

Stick Puppet Patterns

Directions for stick puppets:

Reproduce the patterns on index paper or construction paper. Color the patterns. Cut along the dashed lines. To complete the stick puppets, glue each pattern to a tongue depressor. Use stick puppets with puppet theaters and/or the Readers' Theater script.

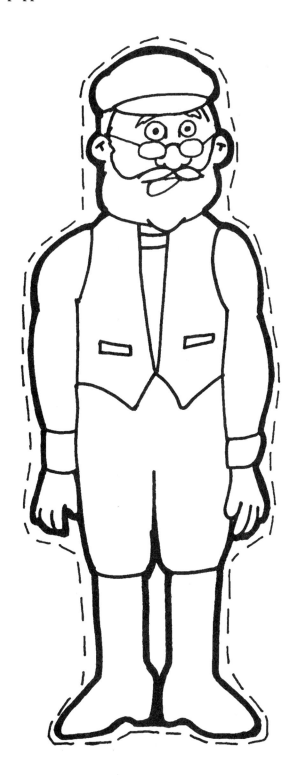

Stick Puppet Patterns *(cont.)*

Stick Puppet Patterns *(cont.)*

Animal Flip Book

Materials needed to make your own flip book:

- four copies of the bottom of this page
- scissors
- crayons or markers
- stapler
- pencil

Directions:

1. Draw an animal's head in the left section, its body in the middle section, and its tail in the right section.
2. Under each section write (1) *WHO* the animal is, (2) *WHAT* it is doing, and (3) *WHERE* or *WHEN* it is doing the action.
3. Follow the same directions for all four pages.
4. Staple the pages together at the top.
5. Color your drawings and cut on the dotted lines.
6. Put a title at the top of your flip book.

1.	2.	3.

Following Directions

This is Peter's house. Follow the directions below to add details to the house and the outdoor scenery.

1. Draw a chimney on Peter's house. Color it red.

2. Draw a door on the house. Color it brown.

3. Draw two windows on the house.

4. Draw a tall tree beside the house.

5. Draw three leaves falling off the tree.

6. Draw the sun in the sky. Color it yellow.

7. Draw three flowers on each side of the house.

8. Color the house yellow.

9. Color the roof green.

Animal Sounds Game

In *Too Much Noise*, Peter was bothered by all the noisy animals in his house. Play this Animal Sounds Game and see if you can match the animal with the sound that it makes.

Directions:

1. Read the names of the animals and the sounds they make.
2. Cut out the cards along the dashed lines.
3. Separate the cards into two piles—one for the animal names and one for the sounds they make.
4. Match the animal with its correct sound.

COW	MOO
DUCK	QUACK
HEN	CLUCK
CAT	MEOW
DOG	WOOF
SHEEP	BAA

Animal Sounds Game *(cont.)*

SNAKE	HISS
OWL	HOOT
DONKEY	HEE-HAW
LION	ROAR
MOUSE	SQUEAK
GOOSE	HONK

You can use these cards for the following games:

- Divide the animal cards into these categories: animals with two legs, four legs, no legs. Or divide them in other ways, such as large animals and small animals.

- Turn all the cards face down on a desk. Play a matching game, such as Concentration. If one player makes a match (an animal with its correct sound), he gets to go again. Two or more people can play this game. The player with the most cards at the end wins.

Leaf Fan

Directions: Cut out the leaf patterns below. On each leaf, print a vocabulary word or spelling **word** from the story *Too Much Noise.* Fasten the leaves together at the stem **with** a brass fastener. Work with a partner. One person reads the word, **and** the other spells it. The words can also be used as flashcards for word recognition.

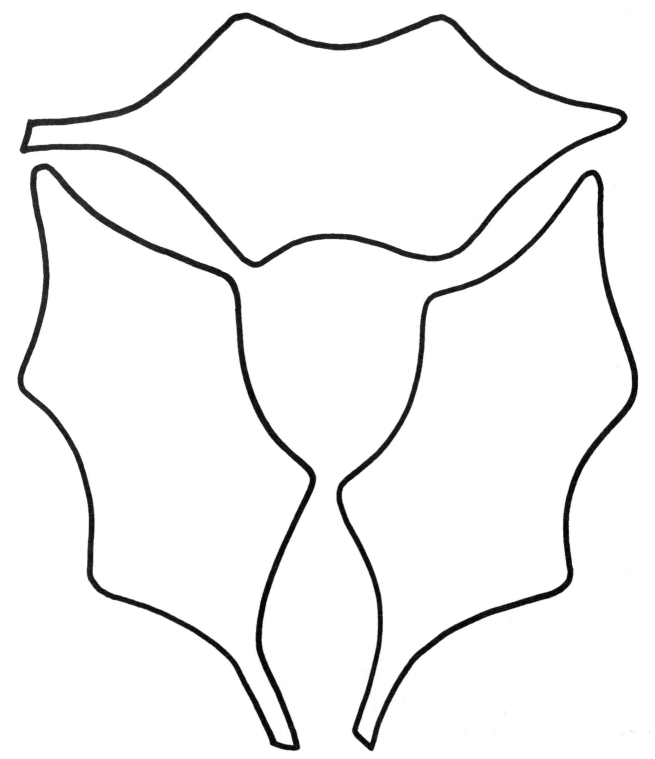

What's Bothering Peter?

Draw or write in the cloud the sounds he hears in his house.

Creating a Story Frame

After reading *Too Much Noise,* complete the following story frame by filling in the blanks to complete each sentence.

This story takes place _____

_____.

_____is a character in the story.

Another character in the story is_____.

A problem occurs when_____

_____ .

After that,_____

_____.

The problem is solved when _____

_____ .

The story ends_____

_____ .

Story Sequence

After reading the story *Too Much Noise,* see if you can recall the events of the story by writing in the clouds below. Begin in the first cloud and write what happened first in the story, then second, etc., going clockwise.

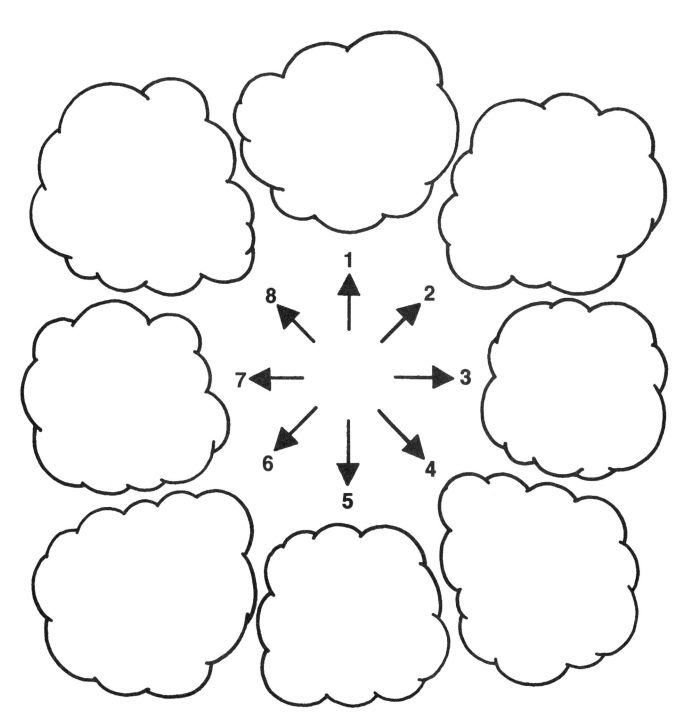

Using Quotation Marks

Teacher Directions: Copy pages 32 and 33 onto tagboard strips for use in the pocket chart. Cut out the boxes. Children must place the quotation marks in the appropriate places in the sentences.

The	cow	said,	Moo, moo!
The	donkey	said,	Hee-haw!
Baa-baa,	said	the	sheep.
Cluck-cluck,	said	the	hen.
The	dog	said,	Woof, woof!

Using Quotation Marks *(cont.)*

Peter	said,	Too	noisy!
Get	a	cow,	said	the
wise	man.	Ah,	said	Peter,
what	a	quiet	house.

"How Many?" Math Problems

Below are some word problems from the story *Too Much Noise.* Read each problem and then solve it in the space provided. Show your work.

---

1. Count how many animals are in the story. Add to that the number of men in the story. How many is that altogether?

2. Ten pigs were in a pig pen. Seven pigs got out. How many pigs were left in the pen?

---

3. Four cows, five sheep, and three goats were eating grass in a field. How many animals in all were eating grass?

4. Six donkeys and five cows were in the barn. Four cows left the barn. How many donkeys and cows are in the barn now?

---

5. Ten leaves fell to the ground by Peter's house. The wind blew five of them away. Then three more leaves fell to the ground. Now how many leaves are on the ground?

6. Peter's house has four sides. Each side has two windows. How many windows are on the whole house?

Teacher's Note: Fold this answer key under before reproducing. If students are to self-correct the problems, do not fold under so students can check answers.

1. 6+2=8
2. 10-7=3
3. 4+5+3=12

4. 6+5=11, 11-4=7
5. 10-5=5, 5+3=8
6. The answer 8 can be arrived at a number of ways.

Science Activities

All Steamed Up!

In *Too Much Noise* Peter's whistling teakettle was hissing and making too much noise. Conduct a science lesson with the class, demonstrating how a whistling teakettle works.

Materials: burner, whistling teakettle, water, tea bags

Directions:

- For safety reasons, make sure children are a good distance from the burner.

- Pour water into the teakettle and place it on a hot burner. After the water starts to boil, ask students what they see coming out of the spout. (steam) What caused the water to change? (heat)

  Explanation: Boiling water turns to steam, which pushes its way up the teakettle spout and through the whistling device. As the steam blows through the opening, the teakettle whistles to let you know your water is ready to make tea.

- Discuss with the class the three forms of water: solid—ice, liquid—water, gas—steam.

Investigating Sounds

The following activities involve demonstrations of sound. Peter thought the few sounds at the beginning of the story were very noisy until he had a house full of animals. Then he knew what noisy really was! Conduct the following experiments with sound and at the same time sharpen your students' listening skills.

Loud and Soft

In this activity one child in the class makes a noise or sound (or claps hands). Add one child at a time until the whole class is making the sound. Notice the difference in the noise level. Tape record the activity so that the class can listen to the differences in noise levels.

Orchestra

Obtain a recording of an orchestra where individual instruments are also featured in solos. Let the children hear the solo instruments and then notice the difference when all the instruments play together.

Alternative: Have eight different children make sounds, one at a time, of all characters in the story *Too Much Noise*—leaves, teakettle, cow, sheep, donkey, dog, cat, and hen. Then have them make all the sounds at the same time. Record the sounds and notice the difference.

Another way to do this same activity is to use instruments instead of voices. These instruments work well: drum, tambourine, wood blocks, recorder, bells, kazoo, and maracas.

Readers' Theater

Readers' theater is an exciting and easy method of providing students with the opportunity to perform a play while minimizing the use of props, sets, costumes, and memorization. Students read the dialogue of the announcer, narrators, and characters from prepared scripts. The dialogue may be verbatim from the book, or an elaboration may be written by the performing students. Sound effects and dramatic voices can make these much like radio plays.

In a readers' theater production, everyone in the class can be involved in some way. The twelve or more speaking parts in this readers' theater combine with the construction of signs and masks to help maximize student involvement. Encourage class members to participate in off-stage activities, such as coloring and cutting out masks, making signs to be placed around speakers' necks, serving tea and cookies, delivering invitations, and greeting guests at the door.

It is not necessary to wear costumes for a readers' theater production, but the students can wear masks, hats, or signs around their necks, indicating their speaking parts. Optional costume additions include the following: Peter, nightcap; Wise Man, a tall pointed wizard's hat; Leaves, some construction paper leaves pinned to shirts; Teakettle, clouds of steam (made from construction paper) pinned to a shirt.

Prepare signs by writing a reader's character (or name of the character) on a piece of construction paper or tagboard. If possible, laminate it for durability. Then, staple a necklace-length piece of yarn to the top of the paper (or punch holes and tie with yarn).

Distribute copies of the following invitation to parents and other guests.

Please Join Us

for Our Presentation of

Too Much Noise

Date: _____   Time:_____

Place:_____

Presented by:_____

Readers' Theater *(cont.)*

Script Booklets

Prepare script booklets for the readers as well. It is well worth the time, and you will have them to use again and again. You will need one script booklet for each reader, including the announcer, the narrators, and the teacher. Highlight (with yellow marking pen) all lines spoken by an individual reader. Write the title and author of the piece being read and the name of the character being highlighted on the outside cover of the booklet. It is a good idea to include all parts in the script booklets. Glue (do not staple) the pages of the script into the booklet and laminate them for durability. Use a long-armed stapler to complete the script booklets.

For a 2–3 page script, construct the booklet as follows:

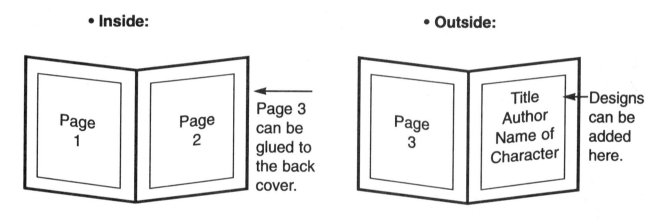

For a 3–6 page script, construct the booklet as follows:

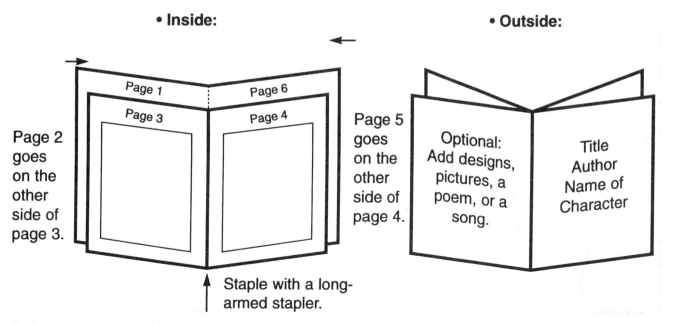

Readers' Theater Script

A Readers' Theater Adaptation of *Too Much Noise*

> **Characters**
>
> | | | |
> |---|---|---|
> | Narrator | Teakettle | Hen |
> | Peter | Cow | Dog |
> | Bed | Donkey | Cat |
> | Floor | Sheep | Wise Man |

Narrator: Once there was an old man named Peter who lived in a very old house. There were noises in that house.

Bed: Creak, creak!

Floor: Squeak, squeak!

Leaves: Swish, swish!

Teakettle: Hiss, hiss!

Peter: My house is too noisy. I will go see the wise man to find out what to do.

Wise Man: Hello, Peter. How can I help you?

Peter: My house is too noisy! The bed creaks, the floor squeaks, the leaves on the roof swish, and the teakettle hisses!

Wise Man: I know how to help you.

Peter: What should I do?

Wise Man: Get a cow, Peter.

Narrator: Peter thought about that, and then he got a cow.

Cow: Moo, moo!

Bed: Creak, creak!

Floor: Squeak, squeak!

Leaves: Swish, swish!

Teakettle: Hiss, hiss!

Peter: Too noisy! I will go see the wise man.

Wise Man: Hello, Peter. How can I help you?

Peter: My house is still too noisy!

Wise Man: Too noisy? Then get a donkey, Peter.

Narrator: So Peter thought about that and then got a donkey.

Donkey: Hee-haw, hee-haw!

Cow: Moo, moo!

Bed: Creak, creak!

Floor: Squeak, squeak!

Leaves: Swish, swish!

Teakettle: Hiss, hiss!

Readers' Theater Script *(cont.)*

Peter:	Too noisy! I will go see the wise man.
Wise Man:	Hello, Peter. How can I help you?
Peter:	My house is still too noisy!
Wise Man:	Still too noisy? Then get a sheep, Peter!
Narrator:	Peter thought about that, and then he got a sheep.
Sheep:	Baa, baa!
Donkey:	Hee-haw, hee-haw!
Cow:	Moo, moo!
Bed:	Creak, creak!
Floor:	Squeak, squeak!
Leaves:	Swish, swish!
Teakettle:	Hiss, hiss!
Peter:	Far too much noise! I will go see the wise man.
Wise Man:	Hello again, Peter. How can I help you?
Peter:	My house is still too noisy! What should I do?
Wise Man:	You should get a hen, Peter.
Narrator:	Peter thought about that and went to get a hen.
Hen:	Cluck, cluck!
Sheep:	Baa, baa!
Donkey:	Hee-haw, hee-haw!
Cow:	Moo, moo!
Bed:	Creak, creak!
Floor:	Squeak, squeak!
Leaves:	Swish, swish!
Teakettle:	Hiss, hiss!
Peter:	Too noisy! I am going back to see the wise man!
Wise Man:	Well, Peter, how can I help you now?
Peter:	My house is still too noisy! What can I do?
Wise Man:	Peter, you get a dog. And, by the way, get a cat, too!
Narrator:	Peter thought about that, and he got a dog AND a cat.
Dog:	Woof, woof!
Cat:	Mee-ow, mee-ow!
Hen:	Cluck, cluck!
Sheep:	Baa, baa!
Donkey:	Hee-haw, hee-haw!
Cow:	Moo, moo!
Bed:	Creak, creak!

Readers' Theater Script *(cont.)*

Floor: Squeak, squeak!

Leaves: Swish, swish!

Teakettle: Hiss, hiss!

Peter: Far, far too noisy! I am angry! I am going to see that wise man and tell him so!

Wise Man: What now, Peter? How can I help you?

Peter: I am going crazy! Too much noise all day long!

Dog: Woof, woof!

Cat: Mee-ow, mee-ow!

Hen: Cluck, cluck!

Sheep: Baa, baa!

Donkey: Hee-haw, hee-haw!

Cow: Moo, moo!

Bed: Creak, creak!

Floor: Squeak, squeak!

Leaves: Swish, swish!

Teakettle: Hiss, hiss!

Narrator: The wise man then told Peter JUST what to do.

Wise Man: Peter, you must let ALL the animals go—the COW, the DONKEY, the SHEEP, the HEN, the DOG, and even the CAT!

Narrator: Peter did JUST what the wise man said. Now he could not hear the . . .

Cow: Moo, moo!

Donkey: Hee-haw, hee-haw!

Sheep: Baa, baa!

Hen: Cluck, cluck!

Dog: Woof, woof!

Cat: Mee-ow, mee-ow!

Narrator: But Peter heard the bed . . .

Bed: Creak, creak!

Peter: How nice—a quiet noise!

Narrator: And Peter heard the floor . . .

Floor: Squeak, squeak!

Peter: Such a nice sound!

Narrator: And Peter heard the leaves on the roof . . .

Leaves: Swish, swish!

Narrator: And Peter heard the teakettle . . .

Teakettle: Hiss, hiss!

Peter: Oh, my house is SO QUIET! I think I will go to bed now and get some rest.

Narrator: And Peter did just that. He slept ever so soundly and dreamed ever so quietly.

Animal Masks

dog

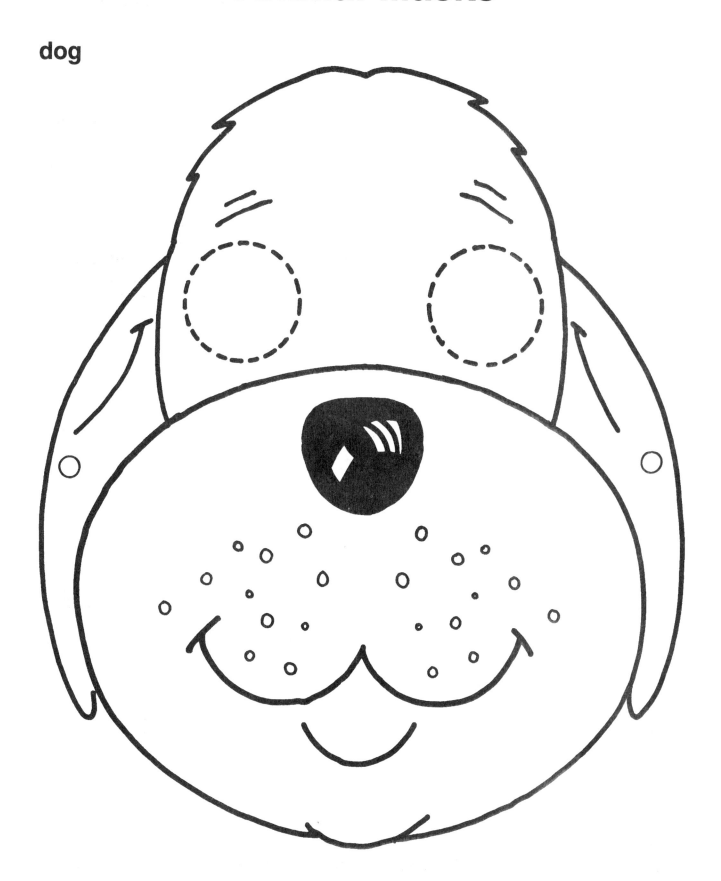

Animal Masks *(cont.)*

cat

Animal Masks *(cont.)*

COW

Animal Masks (cont.)

hen

Animal Masks *(cont.)*

donkey

Animal Masks *(cont.)*

sheep

"Too Noisy!" Bulletin Board

Prepare the following bulletin board at the beginning of the unit. Use it to spark student discussion, to inspire writing, and to focus on a variety of language arts skills presented in the unit.

Materials: light-blue butcher paper; green, red or orange, brown, and white construction paper; construction paper color of choice for border trim; black permanent marking pen; scissors; stapler

Directions:

1. Prepare the background by completely covering the bulletin board with the light-blue butcher paper. Staple around the edges and wherever needed to secure the butcher paper.

2. Add grass to the foreground by cutting a large enough piece of green construction paper to fill the lower half of the bulletin board.

3. Add a construction paper border of your choice.

4. Use a black marker (or create your own letters) to complete the title as shown below.

5. Make an outline of the house on red or orange paper. Cut out the house and staple it to the bulletin board. Add white construction paper windows and a door.

6. Add the tree. Cut out a brown tree trunk and a green top and staple them to the board.

7. Cut out speech bubbles and attach them to the bulletin board.

Variation: At the beginning of the unit, prepare the bulletin board, deleting all labels except the title. Let the class know that they will be reading a new story. As students observe the new bulletin board, ask them what they think the book might be about. As you continue through the unit, add the labels to the bulletin board.

Extensions:

1. At the end of the unit, remove the labels. Have students think of their own sounds or noises that might be used in the speech bubbles. Place them on the bulletin board. Have students use the new information to write their own stories.

2. Create a class big book. The story could involve a character whose house is too quiet, too small, or too large. Together, make a list of ways the situation they selected would affect the character. Use the list and other ideas to develop the new story. Write and illustrate it in a class big book.

Bibliography

Aliki. *My Five Senses.* Harper & Row, 1962.

Bennett, Jill. *Noisy Poems.* Oxford University Press, Inc., 1990.

Branley, Franklin. *High Sounds, Low Sounds.* Harcourt, 1967.

Burningham, John. *Slam, Bang.* Viking, 1984.

Burningham, John, *Sniff, Shout.* Viking, 1984.

Fox, Mem. *Night Noises.* Trumpet Club, 1989.

Gross, Ruth. *The Bremen Town Musicians.* Scholastic, 1974.

Hutchins, Pat. *The Wind Blew.* Puffin, 1986.

Lee, J. Douglas. *Sounds.* Gareth Stevens, 1985.

Leonard, Marcia. *Noisy Neighbors, A Book About Animal Sounds.* Troll, 1990.

Levitin, Sonia. *A Sound to Remember.* Harcourt, 1979.

Mandell, Muriel. *Make Your Own Musical Instruments.* Harcourt, 1970.

McMullan, Kate & Jim. *Noisy Giants' Tea Party.* HarperCollins Child Bks.,1992.

Moncure, Jane B. *Sounds All Around.* Childrens Press, 1982..

Ogburn, Jacqueline K. *Noise Lullaby.* Lothrop, 1994.

Parker, Steve. *The Random House Book of Animals.* Random House, 1993.

Polisar, Barry L. *Noises from Under the Rug.* Rainbow Morning, 1985.

Schmeltz, Susan. *Pets I Wouldn't Pick.* Parents, 1982.

Scott, John Martin. *What Is Sound?* Parents, 1973.

Smath, Jerry. *But No Elephants.* Parents, 1979.

Spier, Peter. *Crash! Bang! Boom!* Doubleday, 1972.

Spier, Peter. *Gobble, Growl, Grunt.* Doubleday, 1973.

Stecher, Miriam. *Max the Music Maker.* Lothrop, Lee, Shepard, 1980.

Strete, Craig. *Big Thunder Magic.* Greenwillow, 1990.

Wells Rosemary. *Noisy Nora.* Dial Bks., 1980.

Witty, Bruce. *Noise in the Night.* School Zone, 1991.

Ziefert, Harriet. *Dark Night, Sleepy Night.* Puffin, 1993.